This Journal Belongs To:

Name _____

Address _____

_____

Phone _____

Email _____

*We hope you enjoyed using this book. It would really help us a lot if you would take a moment to leave a review. Thanks!*

---

*Snippy Chuckles Journals*
*Ha! Ha! Very Funny!*
*Ready for another chuckle?*
*Check out our book catalog at:*

amazon.com/author/snippychucklesjournals

32445102R00062